Sea Level

Sea Level

Poems by SUZANNE MATSON

Alice James Books
Cambridge, Massachusetts

ACKNOWLEDGMENTS

Library of Congress Cataloging-In-Publication Data
Matson, Suzanne, 1959-
    Sea level
      I. Title.
PS3563.A8378S4   1990   811'.54--dc20   90-4952
ISBN 0-914086-84-7

Some of these poems have appeared as follows:
THE AEGEAN REVIEW "Squid," "Your First Questions."   *THE AMERICAN POETRY REVIEW* "Debussy," "There Was a Temporary Accident."   *THE BOSTON REVIEW* "Like."   *FINE MADNESS* "The Artist and His Model," "The Bohemian Wedding," "The Wound-up Girl Ice Skater."   *IRIS* "Woman With Distaff."   *POETRY* "After 'Charming,'" "The Sunbather," "The Sunday Drunk."   *POETRY NORTHWEST* "Fossils," "In Rovaniemi, Finland, Twenty-fifth Birthday," "Love in the Coal Mine," "Newspaper Pictures Out of Poland," "Scotch Coulee," "Widow Aunts."   *THE SEATTLE REVIEW* "Coyotes," "Jackson County Census," "Letters," "Travelers." *SOUTHERN POETRY REVIEW* "Elegy for Neil." ~ *ANTHOLOGY OF MAGAZINE VERSE & YEARBOOK OF AMERICAN POETRY, 1984 EDITION* "The Sunday Drunk." *WORKING CLASS: POEMS ON INDUSTRIAL LIFE* "Love in the Coal Mine."

Book design and typesetting by William Lach.
Cover design by George Sakmanoff and Suzanne Matson.
Cover illustration, "Nude Boy Fishing," is from an Attic Kylix, 480 B.C., courtesy of the Museum of Fine Arts, Boston, H.L. Pierce Fund.

Alice James Books gratefully acknowledges support from the National Endowment for the Arts and from the Massachusetts Council on the Arts and Humanities, a state agency whose funds are recommended by the Governor and appropriated by the State Legislature.

Alice James Books are published by the Alice James Poetry Cooperative, Inc.
Alice James Books, 33 Richdale Avenue, Cambridge, Massachusetts. 02140.

for Kathryn Kaufman Matson

CONTENTS

Drawing Water

FOSSILS

For instance, the way trilobites
work around their past:
they fill and fall in on themselves,
vacancies blooming
into perfect extinct lives.

The shopgirl hugs her arms and stares out,
the tinted day hardly believable.
Customers come, clatters
of square light. She covers
the same steps, backward,
forward. She might leave
before the end of this
to be weather, everywhere, and not
the same twice.

Were we to come after,
sweeping out the empty spaces
she often becomes, we would find her
curled and listening to time,
keeping all that happened,
her getting younger face
swollen like a blank new moon.

WIDOW AUNTS

Widow aunts attending their own funeral
are amazed at how the blue light wasted
into such peony brightness.
They spent the last years fingering beads
like nuns early for vespers:
it was always half-past the buttered lover
with his *kirschwasser* kiss, quarter till the hour
when they must pack away their last good silk.

Now the relatives mill over a farewell drink,
at ease like folded umbrellas,
while among them waft the talcum-fine aunts.
The youngest niece stands stiff in her decorum,
who used to beg to dress up in the old alpaca suit on visits
and come rouged to the breakfast table,
dripping with gem paste and fox tails.

There is just time enough to pour slivered light
into her palm. *Keep it*, the aunts urge,
still in their hats, still swirling smiles and feathers,
You never know when it will come in handy.

DAUGHTERS (I)

> . . . *Out of the murderous innocence of the sea*
> —*Yeats, "A Prayer for my Daughter"*

Slow swells she merely willed through her;
she was waiting to be taken
by something big enough to ring her,
bone china, in some pale Precambrian
silence. It cracked against her,
the surprise of how little she mattered
to it, how it lifted and buried
her, almost wrenching her
apart from what she could think. She
came in on a sheet of foam, still
herself. From somewhere she heard a cry:
It could have been a name, a sigh,
the oath of a murdered father's will
or his violent dream of beauty.

DAUGHTERS (II)

> *May she be granted beauty and yet not*
> *Beauty to make a stranger's eye distraught,*
> *Or hers before a looking-glass. . .*
> —*Yeats, "A Prayer for my Daughter"*

Holding yourself very still like stolen
fruit—My God who is watching you now?
The dream of the Cyclopes keeps returning—
around the stippled apartment it follows

close at heels, relentless as light housework.
Thunder, lightning, thunderbolt: the eyes,
single-minded, starved and humble, stroke
your limbs into a weary kind of pose,

and charge you with their power—even power hid
in your retreat is power. Your own window's
clear-through gaze by day turns black at mid-
night, a mirror for the face outside you,

patient and strange—watching, blank with interest,
your deliberate fists against it.

THE WOUND-UP GIRL ICE SKATER

As long as she doesn't stop she'll be fine.
She is the reason for the long metal arm
stationed at the center of the lake.
It connects to a gear
which is turned by a belt
driven by a small motor beneath Town Hall.
All we can see is the girl, and the arm
rising out of the lake.
Other important signs of the motor
are the beaded lights strung over the Hotel,
Cafe, and Dance Hall, and the milk-white lamps
in their circles of frost on Main Street.
A yellow light gleams from the gable of a splendid mansion:
some papery old soul is sitting up
to trace a psalm, a warming brick
at the end of the bed.

The train skirts town, passes under the bridge, emerges right in the
    center of commerce
and stops at the Depot. Its single freight
is its whistle; to those wrapped in scarves
and poised on porches and street corners—
to all those but the wound-up girl ice skater—
it is a clutch at the throat.
Somewhere they are expected, are they
late? They must go and find what it is that waits for them.
To all, I say, but the girl skater: she understands
circularity, the train's need to keep coming back.
The little townspeople are solid citizens,
they are painted with bright enamel coats and gay smiles.
They stand arm in arm before the shop windows

and look for something. The train returns again,
the town's one grief.

The girl on the arm of the lake goes around much too fast.
She has lost track days ago of days.
She would like to go home for supper;
she can't. She would like to grow up;
she stays nine, with translucent skin. She would like
company; the others huddle together on benches, far
too distant to call to, sipping their hot chocolate.
She would like to remember what it means to be still,
to not move at all, or breathe. Her face
blurs, the tiny blades of her skates don't even touch the ice.
She drills and drills in her own little vortex of present tense
and forgets she was never not this particular girl on skates.

THE SUNBATHER

She is noncommital—faced up flat
like an ornamental slave girl stolen from an Egyptian
frieze, pressed out in imitation of a cat
squeezed into two dimensions.
She smooths black hair behind an ear: the palest
dark flower. Restlessly she rests

with white legs outstretched
on a rose towel spread over the cement,
has for props a pillow, and cigarettes.
She lifts a wrist to catch the scent
daubed there, and lowering the hand,
pauses to feel her ribs through the black band

of swimsuit, as if to make sure of hunger.
She passes fingers down the inside
of a thigh—lifts her eyes to see who saw her,
or didn't. She shifts as the wedge of sun slides
south in the alley under the clothes-
line, follows it, hunching from shadows,

moving her hips an inch
at a time, then shoulders.
But dimness spreads up the ankles—pincers
closing as the pavement grows colder—
even before she found contentment
in a single pose for the only connoisseur present.

THE SUNDAY DRUNK

He sidewinds down the street,
calling his arms and legs back.
It's buck-and-wing into the parking meter
then down to crack his old bone-head on the cement.
Crisp passersby try to mop him up—
but he'll have none of their gauzy good wishes. No,
he'll lie right there as long as they don't
want him to, pooling underfoot,
so that when he finally shakes them loose
their thin soles will go off printing red arrows
in his name. And with that many spare feet
surely he can manage to rise and cakewalk home
in all directions at once: not exactly forward,
not exactly side or back, but something like
a broken box-step
where he wants to go.

VERA

She early learned to make a ceremony
of her beauty. Vera went to town
complete each Sunday, walking her tidy
self like a pedigreed pet. She flowed down
the dry creek bed, its water, in silks, sun-
shade along as her own willful cloud.
Somewhere, she knew, there were bald singing nuns
in churches, or convents, the black-hooded crowd
of them sticking together like seeds
from a melon. *They* might chant and pray
(her heels in smart descant among stones and weeds)
but she had saved her ironing pay
for Kodak picture postcards of her face.
She would save it in albums, mail it someplace.

1880
Moses Ivy, what you knew.
Thirty-four years old, you said
very clearly: 34. White male, laborer,
married to, Gannet? Janet? Jannette?
Did you neglect to spell it out
or did the taker sound out your wife and stumble,
blotting the ink. Children?
Lord yes. Esther, Sarah, Mary,
seven girls by 1880. Moses Ivy you were blessed
with womenkind. Your wife was even then expecting
as she heated the flatiron, eyes
lowered to press out your sleeves and collar,
listening to you shave six years off your life
for the census taker. The girls were stirring
the dinner beans, slicing a loaf, dandling the youngest;
your coveralls slumped in the corner
waiting to be beaten. Moses Ivy,
were you running out of time? Is that why you kept
time in a kind of escrow, compounding
its debt owed you by the world,
past due?

1900
Moses Ivy, sweet Jesus how you
fed on hope. Credit where credit is due.
You traded back a month of faith
for every government acre you turned over.
White male, *sixty*, farmer.
Wife Ganette, gone with the cholera, girls Esther, Sarah, gone off
with husbands, but Mary still stirs your supper.
The new baby was a Nancy, now twenty and turning

every head in the county. Oh, but she's quick and light
and a balm to your new age.
Moses Ivy, you figured right: nothing you get
for nothing; God and the county clerk are reckoners, so you
    squeezed out a little
something to keep by, a pinch of the calendar here and there,
until you finally had time
on your side.

GETTING OUT OF TIJUANA

The border widows come for change,
their fingers wiggling through
inch openings in the car window.

por favor por favor
give me money more beautiful
than all the teeth I have lost

give me money to burn hot holes in my chest,
coins my children will put
in their eyes for silver monocles

NEWSPAPER PICTURES OUT OF POLAND

December 1981

It could have been snowing without moving, just breath.
The half-toned citizens have overturned
another car and it rests with wheels spinning
in the air, its gauges reading full,
meaning empty. Shoppers line up on the sidewalk,
forming a chain of tight grey mouths and mufflers.
One man lies down in the snowy street with his boots on—
perhaps he is just tired, perhaps
his friends are bending to inquire if he is warm enough to sleep.

There is no telling what the figures might do
if allowed to be the next frame.
The car might right itself and drive off to the country
where it will park and wait for the farms to explode
in hard green buds. The shoppers may break apart
and go home, laughing at the prospect of a steaming stew.
Or the tired man's friends might wish to raise him,
thinking to exchange his boots for felt slippers.

But for now in the frozen pictures
snow falls thick, and we know, silent.
Bundled children will have their tongues out, tasting it.

TAKEOVER

The men who came marching in new green jackets
stopped for water and found
plenty. The children advanced
cautiously, as if to a new homeroom assignment,
and saw the men wetting their lips,
then drinking deeply. The mothers froze on the point
of calling the children back, but—
it all happened so quickly—one small girl was taken
by the hand and soon all the children
were settled comfortably in laps.
The mothers began spreading a picnic under the trees.
They recognized their husbands
though the men had grown taller
or shorter, and had changed their language.
Six planes appeared, drawn to the feast like wasps.
They buzzed and dipped
until the women remembered
and tried to hide all the sweet things.
The planes tightened into a V
and flew away—
a silence; a new language.

THE WOMEN ON THE BRIDGE

after Edvard Munch

The women on the bridge are a cinquefoil,
a five-petaled star above
dark water, their foundation.
They meet and clasp hands, nodding
in sunlight. Nothing matters
but them. Together they cast one rose
shadow, which the gentlemen carefully
step around. The gentlemen pretend
an ease, lounging against the guard rail.
They know the women will never return
to their brown-suited selves
and wonder what they can say to each other
after the initial talk of horses
and fine weather. Soon they will drift
home and sit with hats on in dark kitchens
while the women, who are better
than dead, grow less distinct
and finally too bright to watch.

THE ARTIST AND HIS MODEL

after Edvard Munch

Everything moves in the artist's room—
the rug swims like an aquarium
and the palette leaps from the bed.
Every wall the artist assumes
immediately leans, and the vase and table
explode. Nothing is safe from his vision,
not the carpenter's joints,
not the natural light, and not
the model, on whom he concentrates
his narrowest gaze, making her
all seaweed hair and watery chemise.
Beneath the robe her flesh
drips, fades, washes inconsequential
where he will not look.
Her face alone is caught
and held: fills, glows pink
then ruddy, and finally ochre,
her suspicion darkening under the furious strokes
that were her eyes and lips
and now his Work, his own
stilled life.

THE BOHEMIAN WEDDING

after Edvard Munch

Such plenty, such array
of fruit and wine and crockery.
My dear, the bridegroom whispers,
my dear. The bride, that pearl
at the head of the snowy cloth,
makes a mouth.
The guests are reluctant to go home
to ordinary lives,
they toast again and bestow
many friendly pinches.
The bride is thinking of her new house
stuffed with presents: stitched coverlets,
pressed pillowcases, edged napkins—
her last maiden night was spent dreaming
of linens. A swelter of lace!
This new husband's knee is pressing hers.
Here is a critical moment
she knows, and yet what can she do,
she must do nothing.

MARRIED, TO IVAN

Ivan sits unblinking under the inaugural shower
of gold coins. Rock of Russia, over which sheer plenty
will roll away to plant itself

while the old Eisenstein film shows shadows
gouged improbably deep in the white
mask faces. Show glee: glee! Show sorrow: *sorrow.*

The bride Czarina is bundled in her headpiece.
Let husband the Terrible rave about borders and sedition.
What does she care?
She is plump, she is a lily, she is Czarina.
The Terrible will be out mowing death in the fields,
too busy to bother her.
A rose, a peach, a studded egg,
she is garrisoned in blankness.
She sees what she sees, she knows what she knows.
Her eyes roll like tiny coins,
Let her mouth proclaim zero.

WOMAN WITH DISTAFF

In *Tacuinum Sanitatis,* c. 1385, a "Woman
With Distaff Carrying a Basket of Spinach"
heads toward a gate,

neck muscles drawn taut against
the pressure of the basket
she carries on her head. Her dress

is blue plain-stuff, her belly
swells against the white apron at her waist.
No bride's stoic face this, so the swell

and the erect back must be the old habit
of maternity—a pressure that teaches
tautness as response.

Why the heavy lock at the door of the garden?
Does she see the unpicked spinach thrusting knee-high
behind her? The carrying that lies ahead?

And why do the trees grow only taunting
ornaments—unreal red not meant to be
harvested? But she may do it,

in all seriousness, she may, use her tightly wrapped
distaff to beat the symbol trees out of their smug
silence, make it rain red apples
or red plums
out of the paper-white sky.

DRAWING WATER

Italian school, early fifteenth century, "Woman
Drawing Water" kneels before
the well-ropes, her body as fluid as

the cursive letter "f." She's watching the sky
as meanwhile her bucket fills, she hopes,
in the echoing depths where no one can see.

She wears bold lilac in a painted world of ochre,
or perhaps you'd call it burnt sienna,
after the last Crayola crayon anyone would

willingly choose. It is impossible to count
the ochre squashes growing in tumult
behind her back. Not even Thomas

de Cantimpré, who drew her at her drawing,
knows why they are there,
in the land of one color plus lilac,

land of filling gourds
and young arms stretched heavenward
to draw down all she can hold.

Falling Water

AFTER "CHARMING"

> . . . *because charm is like love*
> *the way ice is like water*
> —*William Matthews, "Charming"*

Because to love is to bring water
carried in your hands,
most is squandered along the way,
making it impossible to offer
what you began with.

Because the method is slow and clumsy,
repeatedly not satisfying,
it begins to feel like empty work
only sometimes redeemed
by tripping and losing everything.

And because sometimes the tongue
drinking from the hand forgets
its original want and strays
across the palm to the pulse,
tasting a salt path to the inside elbow,

the original metaphor gets consumed
and love changes.
Because love changes its words,
trimming them expertly and close,
we say the wind has changed around it.

And because we see through the explanation
to its contradiction
the way a tongue can be thirsty and not be at once,

we trace opposites in a breath-clouded mirror
which is another way of not explaining need.

And because need is like love
only half the time, the other half
of love must be different, but not necessarily
opposite, because need has no opposite in language
since language does not name what it does not know.

Though we know ice can't live where water
does, though ice in the hand
is no ice,
because water is either with you or falling,
because falling water always knows where it is falling to.

LOVE IN THE COAL MINE

Once pulled past the black mouth
the girls melted into the sides of their lovers
who knew the slope, the trapdoors, the danger of euphoria.
Unbuttoning the descent with a flashlight
wasn't like choosing a hollow on the beach
where open sandstone cliffs could be your temporary fort
and white light poured through gaps in the blankets.

Love in the coal mine, though damp and hot,
wasn't like wrapping legs around your love in Lost Lake—
him standing your sliding ground,
you leaning back to float your hair on the water
like a slip of woodsmoke. And underground
you could never find anything like a pair of quick tongues
cricketing by a campfire.

Down there it was a deathless weight
rolled over your eyes, a thickness
that filled your throat, making lungs grow ragged
like an untimbered ceiling. In the breathless rooms
you could believe in a flickering out—
the way stiffening vertebrae arch and rise
in the underbellied dark.

NEWS FROM THE FIRE STRIP

If there were a fire, news from here
would be inaudible, shouts mustered
through speaking tubes of air so burnt
that each word crackled like spittle over hot rocks.
We wave to the distant people
who wave back, cheerfully.
Just out of reach colored flags are waving
and flowers crack apart like guilty smiles.
The outside world keeps promising itself to us—
cheeks of milk-blue sky floating in the breakfast porcelain,
the teeth of admiring moonlight clinking in crystal.

We are hungry as ever—
just the wish to keep taking things in.
Our hearts swing into lockstep.
We have a song, it repeats,
it passes through us like bars of shadow from a circling plane.
We are learning our occupation: we occupy,
pat the ground to remember it,
count hours from our plain and only business,
which is here, to be
as here as we can be—
in our devouring body, with a vengeance.

THE GOOD MORNING

Something crosses his look—
a brief animal distress, or a man's fear
of being followed out into the morning
of clean round breaths and brisk
leather soles on the sidewalk.
He walks loosely, long-limbed
to his car, fingers the change floating
in his pockets, and breaks
into a smile—for all of it, this
fog burning off over the bridge, this warm
rosy woman he has left at her door, still
searching him, her hands
moving under his coat, buttoning and unbuttoning him,
everywhere smoothing him.
He drives smoothly over the bridge;
he does not suppose that his mouth may have twisted slightly
at the door, that she saw,
or that he made a tiny motion to push
her back in, as though she would want to persist where cold
was so wide and bright and obviously his.
He hums over the bridge
and will soon let himself through his own front door.
A sheet of light slips in with him
like a pet belonging to this big house.
The thermostat clicks to prove the silence that kept
for him, dust motes flicker in the hall.
He's home, and always was.
He grinds beans for coffee, black and fragrant,
lifts the rattle of steam from the kettle, and sees
that morning has followed him now to the kitchen,
coming through the window, rose-blue.

RIDING THE LAST ROW OF THE ARTICULATED BUS

Is it centrifugal or centripetal?
I daydreamt through the naming
of physical forces in tenth grade.
Now, swinging like the gutteral note
an alto sax makes, I'm all the way back
to Saturday mornings at Oaks Park Roller Rink
where I scuffed through backwards and forwards practice
just to be in the whip at the end of the hour; me
always the trailing tongue of resistance, fearing
to be catapulted over the side, but loving
to skitter across the widest part of the arc. The harder
the swing the more strain
on our fiercely gripping sweaty hands. And so what
if I turn out to be the casualty
that spins loose, *D. C. al fine*
to some molar-shattering end?
It's the ride, after all;
it's the speed with which you're propelled
sideways over surprising ground
that makes being let go
small price.

WANTING, THE MORTUARY

In particular, I want to touch it, the grey
somebody who is only his name and shirt size,
dressed dignity and a fresh carnation.

I once saw a picture of a man propped up
on fluted satin, the newspaper in his hands open
to his obituary. He wore reading glasses
at the correct angle to see; someone must have thought
he would need convincing.

My love and I made a pact
to read from *The Book of the Dead*
for whoever goes first. At the moment
when we hover undecided between
the deceiving colors of this world
and the pure dark of the next,
we are to listen to the firm voice
reading in our old body's ear—
Giant step, Giant step, now Scissor.
It couldn't hurt.
Then we'll wait for each other, shining,
even if late begins to seem like forever.

LETTERS

1

In our favorite cafe, tables jumbled
back to back, I watch you watch
others, your problem always
faces—*that guy, what does he do?*

The man makes two arrows
with his hands. They are going
to meet. His friend nods, yes
it is quite clear, he understands completely.
Where did they learn such symmetries?
Beards wag, followed by two short reports
of laughter. Now the man's hands
drift apart, emptied of climax
and the flare of a match
he paused to shield.

2

You were hands by the river,
that is how I knew you,
one palm flattened
over my left breast.
Every time you feel my heart
you tell me, and every time
it is a new wonder.
Pressed by you, I know myself
to be alive
though under perpetual cover.

3

We lay under a cover of stars,
their evoked fire,
our stunned separation.
And if stars seen from earth
are already bodies of absence, why do they
make me think how close,
how intensely personal? Again you ask
what I'm thinking, only this
time it was nothing, really nothing.
Only the vast resistant space
between morning and meeting you
again.

4

We must have been strangers once.
We must have passed on this street
as invisibly as the new faces passing now,
each designing threat with promise: look
too closely and our natural distance will collapse
until, under the pressure
you begin to feel a familiar heart beating.
It arrives like a consolation,
what we have in common,
the countless subversions
of ourselves, ourselves, ourselves.

COYOTES

They never grew bodies
but came as a howling we couldn't fix
  from the direction of the woods, the fields,
  the flank of heavy hills.

A party of yelps that could have been tavern gaiety
  or baby slaughter: the impossibility of knowing
  them, bounded by our own interpretations.

We waited from the porch, tobacco and drinks
  to keep us human,
and listened to them take shape
  on the dark grid of space, their rise
  in inverse proportion to the subsiding house,
  lights extinguished, children sleeping.

The longer we sat up, the more we were absorbed:
  the house a mute, scarcely separate
  terrain, our smells no different than wind.

They crept closer,
  and in various forms: a single throat
  opening itself in the field,
  or a small chorus of barbed cries from the trees.

Clouds whitened the sky
  then slid open
  leaving us helpless to the moon—
  all our plaints for it inarticulate,
  a trajectory of yearning
  that begins and ends with ground.

VENETIAN MOSAIC

1

This is the day when we will
do something irrevocable; I know this
in advance. I knew this the last time
our talk turned dusk then dark,
I knew this in the days of heavy rain
intervening. I knew it when the sun
came out this morning and I bought tulips
you would see and opened the kitchen window.
You rested your hand flat on the windowsill
to feel its warm and cold and flaking paint
and soot. The knowledge is sharp enough
when dark comes again
and you reach out your hand
in the manner of saying goodbye.

2

Goodbye to space as something.
Now we face its opposite,
no space at all between us.
Now you stand to go and there must be
some part of me touching until you step out
into this newly safe world.
You will carry it across the country
and still there is no space.
This is as surely as if
we had become lovers.
Urgency is out of the question.
I am sure I have been touched,

willing myself through something
more formal than air.

3
I am trapped in the hour
of becoming new to you.
Where we make the same gestures, and speak
the same words, till I want
to let new minutes in like rain.
Come back, come in.
The body is alone
around a brand new absence
of its own unmaking,
standing in perfect self-sufficiency,
loving to be multiplied into love.

4
In Venice, where we didn't go,
the streets are dripping with tentacles
and sea water and gold. Out of the fragments
I can hold us still
unyielding, composed, young,
blameless. I can lead
our artful, brilliant lives.

THERE WAS A TEMPORARY ACCIDENT

the
story

Find me you said
so I walked between the large
hotels, Broadway, Times Square,
and liked walking there liked
the low growls by me on the sidewalk
the grit under my dress
the fear of dirty water
for adults only the sex
blinking on and off,
marched across the intimate sour
smell of the subway grates
coming to be admitted
to do anything you wanted
just to see you want

I kept back the word because the word
was everything
perishable to air—
viral multiple dying resistant—
making itself over a thousand ways,
selfish as the word
on the lips of the sucking
mouth. It was the word I
could never allow out
knocking against my ribs
as you—

What is never said grows large
in interest
a speculation
its numeral glint round as a zero—
two faces rapt darkly in a locket

trapped staring not saying,
the violence of the untold story reduced to
a word, a palmable heart
small enough to swallow
without bodily harm

(I said have more, your fill,
licked your teeth to get you to bite)

the
real
story

A) The man surprised himself by hitting
the bus
he is weeping.
The bus was there and
his car was there and
his post-surgical heart said
don't stop, kiss
metal feel
the substantial blunt fact
moving in front of you

B) There was a temporary accident
the woman ran into the man
holding the knife.
She bleeds, she doesn't realize
as she looks in the mirror
wondering about her face
if it is the one she remembers, if
it has anything to tell
her. She discovers then
how much she has
bled, what

was dumb about the face, the red
lips, how blood follows
laws of water, leaving like
words the mouth had hoped
to say, blood, love, heart's desire,
words the mouth
lost in the floods:

DEBUSSY

Most of the night it rained
while the small soprano sang French.
I didn't understand although I never doubted
how right it all must be.

Most of the night it rained
and there was little I could do
to convey how sorry I was
how surprised at the laundry's
white returning drift
how right that the singer sang
what was only almost so close

and what was wrong was
so little really, when examined.
How fine I felt at the end.
How ripe, in all, my position   *(resistance)*
                                        (willingness)

NULLIPARA

Only your name now—
that marble dislodged,
thundering across the floor—
your name now the shuddering
loose of shape
shape my tongue
has practiced, you
the name now rolling
in the dim zone before
sleep where there is no
narrative, no
plan, no sense
of the next thing or even
an end, just
the hollow of name,
your name now doubling
and tripling as though
it were a sign of something
or a route to somewhere
or had the properties of
charm and safety
that were a death,
a multiplication of heaven.

LIKE

We'd only just lie touching
at the hips, the heels,
your big flat palm flat on the back of my hand like
liking itself, the weight outside that impresses,
taking your own as its measure
as you measure you by it, as as
takes two, like like,
like the way a word never finishes,
or says goodbye,
just so long.

Some Seas

VALISE

The words of travel, *valise*, for example.
What couldn't you pack into
it? Where couldn't you
take it? Better than Florence,
the ticket to, urgency leading you through
queer fresh stale air in the station;
newspapers damply waiting to be cut free
from stacks. The imperative of the last
rush to a mailbox, your final word from here
before you become unreachable, utterly.
Then you have it, the sleek
carbons of your exit:
one for now, one for there,
one as the faint but non-negotiable reminder
of where you've been.

YOUR FIRST QUESTIONS

How much does that cost?
The rug, dyed the color
of crushed poppies,
color sheared from the rocks and roots
and combed into a long hall runner.
I will unroll it down a dark corridor
glowing in an invisible house
I am returning to.

I want to make a phone call to the invisible house
across the pictures I hold
and the pictures they hold
and the silently roaring place between
where I twist in my bedsheets,
an engine of useless adrenalin
fueled by dreams where they show themselves,
briefly.

What time is it please?
My clock ran backwards as I slept
and when I awoke it started ticking
in place, one second forward, one back.
Next door at the church the silver-bearded priest is hanging
on the bell-ropes, but in my shuttered room
there is no light, no time.
The body in the dream keeps its face hidden.
All over the island neglected clocks point
to a different stilled hour.

May I borrow your pen?
I have bought beautiful scenes
of the island: priests in their dark
robes and hats climbing the stone steps,
sheep fat and yellow against the hill,
villas with plenty of sky. The old women bend double
over their looms, poppies sprout among the rocks and roots.
I will add my love and address;
I will conjure myself among the dreamed.

PHRASES FOR PROBLEMS

What do you think is wrong?
They are kneeling in the dust by the side of the road,
they are examining the tires.
The old man knows his son will fix everything,
it is what he raised him for, this:
so he can sit on a rock in his next best suit,
unshaven and with slitted eyes, his pleasure
to watch the tight bulging in his son's shirtsleeves
as the young man leans cursing into the bolts.

My son is lost. I saw him last
as he ran ahead with the dog he found,
scattering beach gravel from his heels,
the flashing of his small tanned calves.
I lost him around the bluff
where he disappeared into the next cove.
When I caught up there was only the Greek child
throwing stones into the waves
to make his dog whine and bark with excitement.
The dog didn't run into the sea,
no one ran into the sea,
and the stones sank to the bottom
from where they will return, in time.

That man keeps following me.
He began it in Paris, where I found him
at my elbow in the Place St. Michel
smiling and ready to talk to me in any language at all.
Now I see him dogging me on the island, keeping
a discreet distance away, raising his hand
to signal. If I pause in the square by the war memorial
I'll see him leaning against the stonecut names of the resisters.

What do you want? he asks me.
Nothing at all, I say.
Sure? he smiles.

I have broken a glass.
I have spilt something.
Behind me they call for more glasses, trembling to the lip
with the island *kokkineli.*
I call for octopus, salad, bread.
No one has noticed the dark stain
spreading from my shadow to the sea.

SQUID

The way to eat squid is to catch it first,
best if you pull it out of the dripping net yourself,
a gift you didn't ask for from among the ordinary
bone-filled catch you did, and the purple sea-stars, inedible
bad luck you didn't deserve.
Next to eat squid you waste a fire
to coals, nestling the flaccid bodies
into the earth for as long as it takes, usually
long. Finally you may eat the small charred
legs, one by one, working your way
to the ink-filled heart. This is a shared
humiliation, and at this stage you are obliged
to press your lips to any nearby lover,
mark him as indelibly as you can.

TRAVELERS

So you have been wandering again father,
out of your room to exchange
your hats in other closets,
napping vaguely in familiar beds.
When the elevator moves you believe
you have caused it,
counting it as a success
as you lower yourself to the dining hall
where the other resident waits for his ride up.
How well you know you can't go on like this.
The Home at night assumes
the proportions of a church
or a weirdly echoing train station
or the most famous ballroom you ever danced in,
if only you could say where.
Now late and thirdhand news from across the ocean
tells me you won't be allowed to stay.
In this scrubbed and German-founded Home
you wear your own trousers, period.
Me, I'm moving with you Papa
through foreign states.
We clutch some bags and lose others.
We practice our sentences
though the careful crystals we make of them
shatter in air and anyway are finished too late to help.
We keep a lookout and we hope we will recognize
the rooms we leave.
We guard our purses because once we lose them
we can't prove a thing.
These nights we tend to cry at the drop of a hat.
These nights we sleep with friends
and wake with strangers.

SCOTCH COULEE

There was no one from the old crowd to greet him,
only the creek thinned and blue
like a collapsed vein.

It had taken three wrong turns to arrive;
my father finally splayed his hands out, witching
for the nameless dirt fork to Scotch Coulee

as if collecting a debt the sagebrush owed him
or reading a magnetic code held coiled
in his cells for sixty absent years.

And if the very ground remembered him, the walls
had broken their appointments
down to the skeletal grey timbers; but a sign

nailed to the abandoned pumphouse said *build to suit*
so he worked foundations up around me, piecing together
the Oukalas, Hakkinens and Andersons from the lay of their
      cornerstones.

This is the way we walked to the mine, he said
pointing to the white company houses
left behind in one-quarter light.

This is the way we walked—
swinging lunch buckets weighted with *pastie*,
silent Finns together, Austrians and Swedes ahead.

And this must be the kitchen window
where the women leaned above the breakfast dishes
dreaming it lighter and lighter over the hills, sending

jaunty feathers of blue light
to float and bob with their men underground,
the women busy twisting

tight braids to lead them home again—
braided rugs, braided hair, braided bread.
I shall be my father's mother, take her seat

here in this rocker, sip a last dish
of coffee through a sugar cube
and watch her sixth and middle child bid

goodbye to the confetti rag rugs
goodbye to the scoured wood floors,
see him mark the last ten paces to the sunlit door.

IN ROVANIEMI, FINLAND, TWENTY-FIFTH BIRTHDAY

Up where light hesitates,
    starts late,
then floods the snow and gleaming
    modern housing—
the clustered village streets,
    where, quiet,
shops are full of unused
    goods, raised
hopes are all: electric
    appliances thick
with six months' dust, the stuff
    of civilization; enough
to know it's there.

At Ounasvaara, a small hill outside
    of town, made
into a sports resort, but empty
    now, ski
trails shining under sun,
    in silence, mine.
Not silence: the rhythmic scruff
    of skis on snow, and breath
loud in my ears, the effort
    to be effortless,
transform the work to pendulum,
    ride momentum;
as far as possible, be air.

Time at the top was no time.
    If now I'm
older, time turned in too wide

a place to know, the light
unconvincing, unconvinced,
    a hinge—a sense
of something further: what? Then,
    not alone,
birds startle, thump to flight
    from under white
bramble-flurry; shapes too swift
    to name have lifted,
leaving wing-flash, and emptier air.

In time I'm on the train again,
    the minutes leaden
before leaving, baggage stowed
    above my head.
The stationmaster whistles, flags us out,
    we start:
one lurch, then rolling
    from world-end falling
back to tracks, a film rewinding
    as backwards riding
I watch my progress disappear—
    the trees are thicker,
light lasts longer; I'm headed somewhere.

FOR MY MOTHER ON HER BIRTHDAY, SWIMMING

In water, where you are drawn
time and time again, you are
happy, though still perhaps not completely
yourself. You kick too hard at the surface,
you slice the water with straight arms.

There were days I can faintly remember, brave
lessons you gave yourself in letting go
of the rope, the sides, talking yourself into the deep
end as if your life depended on it.

Only now can I conjure up your fear, your will.
Those days, in my childish element, I swam somersaults
beside you, circles around you, had enough breath left over
to laugh while you did your Red Cross paddling, chin thrust
up, mouth not my mother's fuschia lipsticked, but a woman's
silent "O" of effort.

Untaught, I threaded the turquoise
like a silver animal
and if I could now
I would go back and reinvent the moment someone
showed you how to be afraid, promised dark things
of deep water, and made you hug the shore.

ELEGY FOR NEIL

When Neil sits at his strawberry ice cream
of an evening, his ninety years melting
through him, his dead wife serving always serving

I am at my desk in the city sealing
a note, preparing to go out, the dress
pressed and hanging on a hook, shoes paired

like the couple that drifts conspiritorial
beneath my window—that invisible
bond joining the shoulders of the long-married.

Neil spoons the last drop thoughtfully. He knows
he will return to his house after this
illness. Ghost of his wife, ghost of garden,

ghosts thick in the air between my old
home and my new. I hardly knew the man.
Yet what I know as the unknown couple

slips from sight is how little we are ever
alone: as the barometer falls around us all
tonight, the frost that scalds the morning glass
is the intricate map of love.

CEREMONY

To hear this music I have dressed with care,
have pulled the ritual pieces from their drawers—
fine stockings, old brooch, a band for my hair.
I am clean like mint. For these hours
when early night and scouring cold conspire
we will gather in a lit place, restless
until the conductor lifts the thin wire
of our attention. Another man directs us.
I love the maestro's fine hands, all the rapt
taut beauty he shapes in air, cutting loose
our small private lives so they may rise, rise, locked
together in an abstract joy like prayer.
I need a Father, need a God, and fear
the need. No matter. Though close, He is not here.

TO HER FRIEND THE PHYSICIST

You at least have a language for your uncertainty: and principles
you stack like cordwood behind the shed.

I attach the shed to a house and by the time
this line breaks off in your infinite space
I have peopled the house with my ancestors, or
yours, and they are already quarreling over my mis-
representations of them, who it was really
that ran off with his sister. Sometimes I think it a sin
to handle relations as I do, reading disappointment and desire
in every date of marriage, birth, and death, looking outside
the border of the photograph for the handsome young
photographer making the pair of sisters smirk.

Sometimes I think it a sin to handle relations as you do,
as airy math, a lattice of abstraction
that moves through us without touching—
our very bodies elementary sums.

And then I think how similar
our taste for the invisible,
the *primum mobile* of our calendar
of days. Our formal love betrays
us into faith; though some impossible
night is sure to fall without us—
unaccountable, erased.

HOME AND OTHER FUTURE TRAVEL PLANS

Parting the clouds at 25,000 feet, your face
a midge in the sky, Modern Moses,
you leave to talk about home.
Later you will come back to talk about having
left, leaving again.

Only here, en route, are you momentarily
safe enough, leaving and returning
distinguished only by the film that plays east
versus the film playing west.

You're not lost, you're in possession, home
as known as the back of your hand, while your
travel futures lay coiled in your film,
needing only exposure,
naming, editing, narration:

This is where we bought the rug,
This is where we ate the goat,
This is where we inexplicably sickened,

and This—after the accidental gap in the sequence
that leaves you blinded by projection—

This is where we really thought of settling down.

DAUGHTERS (III)

> *O may she live like some green laurel*
> *Rooted in one dear perpetual place.*
> —*Yeats, "A Prayer for my Daughter"*

In my temporary furnished room
overlooking the broad avenue
custom and ceremony are the same
as they were a hundred years ago.

November rains strip the deep-rooted trees
of leaves, making home a place the heart
advertises to itself, a lee-
ward angle of the mind: "at home" the art

of making safe a place, imagining
a ground you hold unto yourself, while it,
one wishes, cleaves to you. Holding something
with this faith is tantamount to love. And yet,

love is also in the life you pack,
bearing solid acquaintanceship to lack.

AMBERGRIS

There is a time to hunt for ambergris,
but I do not know it. It must be past,
ages past, that women walked, hatless
into suns so low that hope of light lasting
very long past supper was slim—at best
the promise of a stroll to ease the stiff
and overfed, the wakeful party of guests
assembled on a wide white porch. Don't love
too well the scene: the girl's shawl luffing,
her young man at his ease, but barely, his
fingers twining secretly the tress
he would romantically call goldenness
itself. Summer's done. And ambergris,
a fixative, is said to be found on some seas.

POETRY FROM ALICE JAMES BOOKS